Scattered Emotions
An Assortment of Poetry
By Sky Boivin

Other books:

An Assortment of Poetry
Scattered Emotions
Inspired Thoughts
Random Thoughts
Something Loved
Anger Withheld
A Twisted Vine
The Alice Poems
Faye Love Poems
A Moon Filled Song
Thoughts To Be Had
A Natural Way
Beyond Time
Faded Memories

Also:
Their Hope Within The Flames
Life Without You
The Sisters Two Chronicles:
    The Queen Faye- beginnings
Short Story Teasers

Horizon Before Me

I was standing in my own storm,
Before you came into my life,
By then,
I had decided to leave my old ways.
[NO MORE PAIN]
I had decided to get away from the prior situation.
[I DESREVE BETTER]
I separated the huge storm
into smaller storms;
pushing the troublesome one away.
Standing in my own storm,
I notice the sun shining before me.
A stranger from past thoughts
Appeared in the horizon.
Was it just a dream?
Every time I talk with you,
I think more and more that maybe you
were that stranger trying to help me before.
The only difference is that now you are here.
And all I can say is
Thank you for finally coming into my life.
I am glad that Destiny finally sent you to me.

11.21.2000

Yesterday

I wish that I could go back to yesterday.
Before everything happened.
I wish they would stop playing
That horrible event on the news;
Over and over again.
Isn't it bad enough,
That I myself cannot seem to stop
Replaying it over in my head?
Every time I stop in my tracks
To think about something,
My mind always falls back to that day.
To that one moment in time.
Watching live as the Twin Towers
Got slammed by two planes.
Then, hearing that they have crumbled
Like a deck of playing cards that someone
Was trying to make into a house.
Again, I ask,
Will we ever be allowed
To return to yesterday?

9.20.01

Everyone's Hero

Everyone is always looking for a hero.
"Look to the common man," Wordsworth would say.
Is not that exactly what has been happening?
Since a freak day on September 11, 2001,
Hundreds of people lending a hand.
The terrorists wanted to stop us all,
To make us like the poet at his last.
But instead, we are like the leech-gatherer.
Standing in the pile of muck and rubble
of our beloved Twin Towers.
In the pile of our lost loved ones and friends.
The common fire fighters and police officers lost,
And passengers on the planes,
They are the true heroes.
Heroes are of all shapes and sizes.
Don't be discouraged anymore.
Who else could be a hero?
Any one, it could be you or me.
Just be brave, and do your best.

10.9.2001

Sister Whispers

Silent whispers in the night,
Moving bells without ringing,
I remember this of you.
'can you make it across the room without it ringing?
If so, then you pass the test.'
What test was this for?
You never had the chance to tell me.
For I was "whisked away" from you suddenly
And without warning.
You could not stop it from happening.
Neither could I.
The Fates had other plans for me.
We had to be separated
So that I could find my way.
But what way was that?
To learn to listen to myself?
To be myself?
Instead of maybe living in your shadows?
Could that have happened?
If I had stayed?
Who really knows.
Only the Fates do.
And that is why they do what they do.
I was destined to go with my mother.
To learn the teachings of that side.

Alone.
To be led back to you,
And my other sisters at a later time.
The Fates work in wondrous and mysterious ways.

3.25.2004/4.14.2013

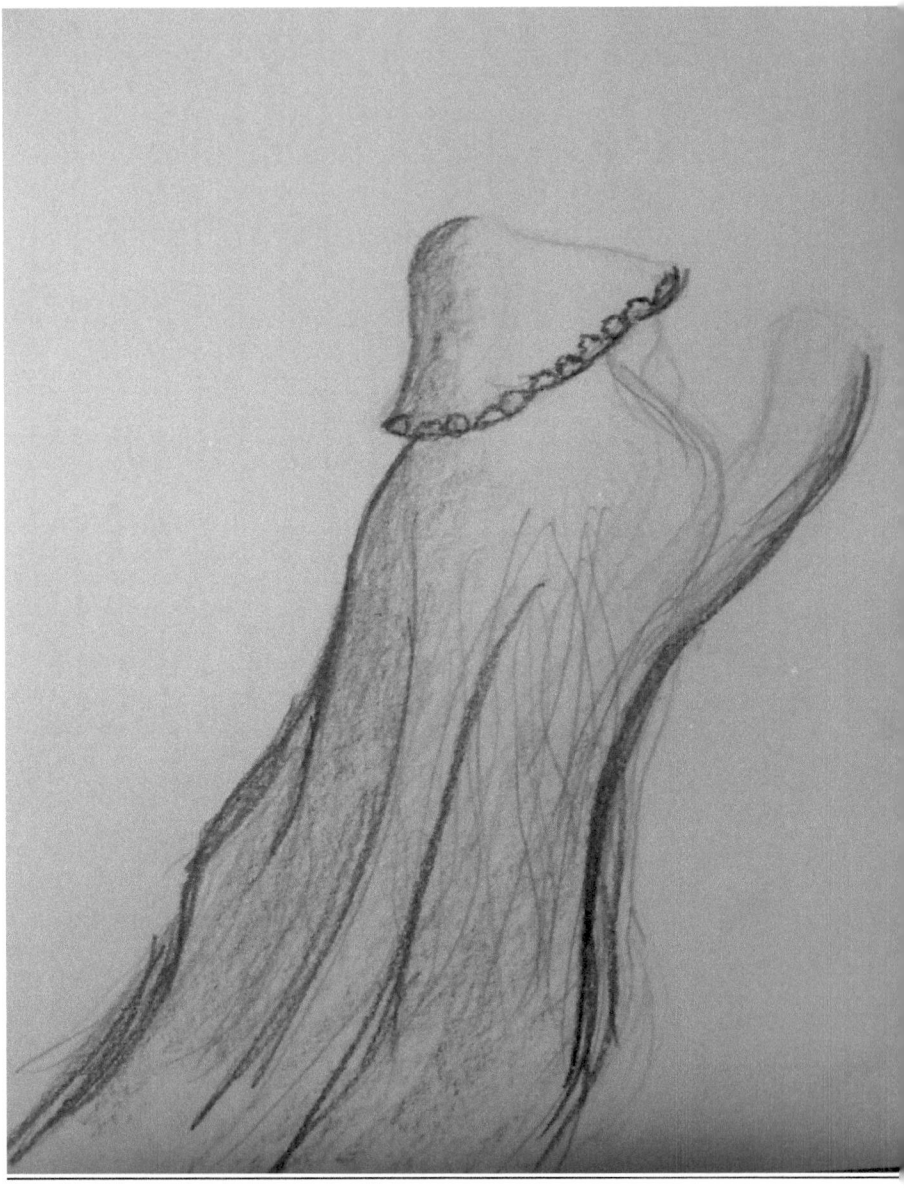

That Head of Yours

What was going on through your mind?
All those years?
As you led me on.
Pretending to be my friend.
What was going on through that thick head of yours
When we hung out all those years.
Was I just a toy?
Was I really just a thing of amusement to you?
A doll you can just fling away,
When you grow tired of it?
Is that all I was to you?
What had possessed you to just cut ties that we had?
Did you enjoy yourself all those years
That you wasted of mine?
I admit,
It did hurt then.
Slightly hurts still today.
What you did to me.
But I ask you one final time,
What was going on through that head of yours?

10.4.2004

Small Heroes

A small blonde sits upon the bench.
She's been watching all season.
She holds a pen in her hand.
She scribbles frantically
On a small piece of paper.
"Go Westie Go
Go Katie Go
Go Nikki Go"
She climbs over to me,
"mommy, who else?"
So I write on the back,
'Jess, Kate, Smitty'.
Someone else helps her with the rest.
She climbs off the bleachers
And runs to the fence.
She's made a small banner
For her softball heroes.
She cheers, even at the very end.
While medals are being passed around.
She still looks up to her Dudley heroes.

7.24.2006

To Michelle

Almost a year ago.
Ages, it seems.
That you departed from us.
A year ago we found out,
That you were ill.
Swept through you,
Weeks, barely.
Expected,
Yet unexpected it was.
Waiting. Agony for the day.
Heart torn in half still to this day.
Some songs and thoughts,
I still cry.
You are still alive
Every time I help others.
Fundraising,
City of Hope, Med City for kids,
Teaching Brownies to live by "The Law".
You are still around.
I hear your whispers upon the wind.
And I know you are near.

11.13.2006

Wind in the trees

Wind in the trees,
Wind in my hair.
Words down on paper
That I write here.
Wind rustles the bushes,
Wind ruffles my paper.
Children's chatter I hear afar.
Bird song in the wind,
Chill on the breeze,
As I sit writing here.
Quiet, calm, and peaceful
With the scent in the air.
Wind in the trees,
Wind in my hair,
Carries the sweet smell
Of rain in the air.

5.2.2007

Goblin King

Goblin King you call to me.
I dare not go.
Sweet dreams you send to me.
I dare say no.
Your eyes capture me,
Your voice commands.
Yet, and yet I still dare say,
"You have no power over me."
Goblin King keep up your games
But they will still be in vain,
For my free spirit
Is powerful still to resist
The Goblin King.

5.2.2007

The Severed Link

I do not hear your whispers
Upon the wind
Any more.
Why is that?
Have you disappeared entirely?
Have I lost my connection?
It scares me
To think it may be so.
But, at the same time,
If you have moved forward
And I have gone on the road
You have hoped for me.
Then your job is done
And you are free.
If it is the later,
Then how do I
Reconnect
The Severed Link?
To be able to hear
Any whispers from anyone anymore?

4.14.2013

Breaking Point

I held you when you hit the wall.
I shared in your tears.
I felt the pain.
I understood.
I saw my mother hit that same wall.
That was many years ago.
Now, it is your turn.
You have hit that wall.
That Breaking Point.
Now, is the time to heal.
It may not be easy.
But, you will get through it.
My mother did, and so will you.
You need to reach your Breaking Point,
Before the Healing can Begin.

9.11.2013

The Song of September Eleventh

It is hard to believe that it has already been twelve years.
Where has the time gone to?
It really does seem like it was just yesterday.
So surreal it all was.
Watching the plane go into that second tower.
Everyone recalls where they were on this day,
Twelve years ago.
Ages ago.
It still brings tears to my eyes,
To see the photos in memorial of the Twin Towers.
They range from lights in place or flags in place of the two towers.
All I can think of is how sad
That day was for all those lost.
Lost innocent souls snatched too soon from us.
Also, how lucky we were that others were still safe.
Ranging from a father stranded
Across the country.
Having to hitch hike back home.
To calling through to Virginia
Because of a cousin working at the pentagon.
All around, all is on edge for any new news about the day.
All praying for good to come crawling up out of all the bad.
All we can do is bury the past and continue on.

9.11.2013

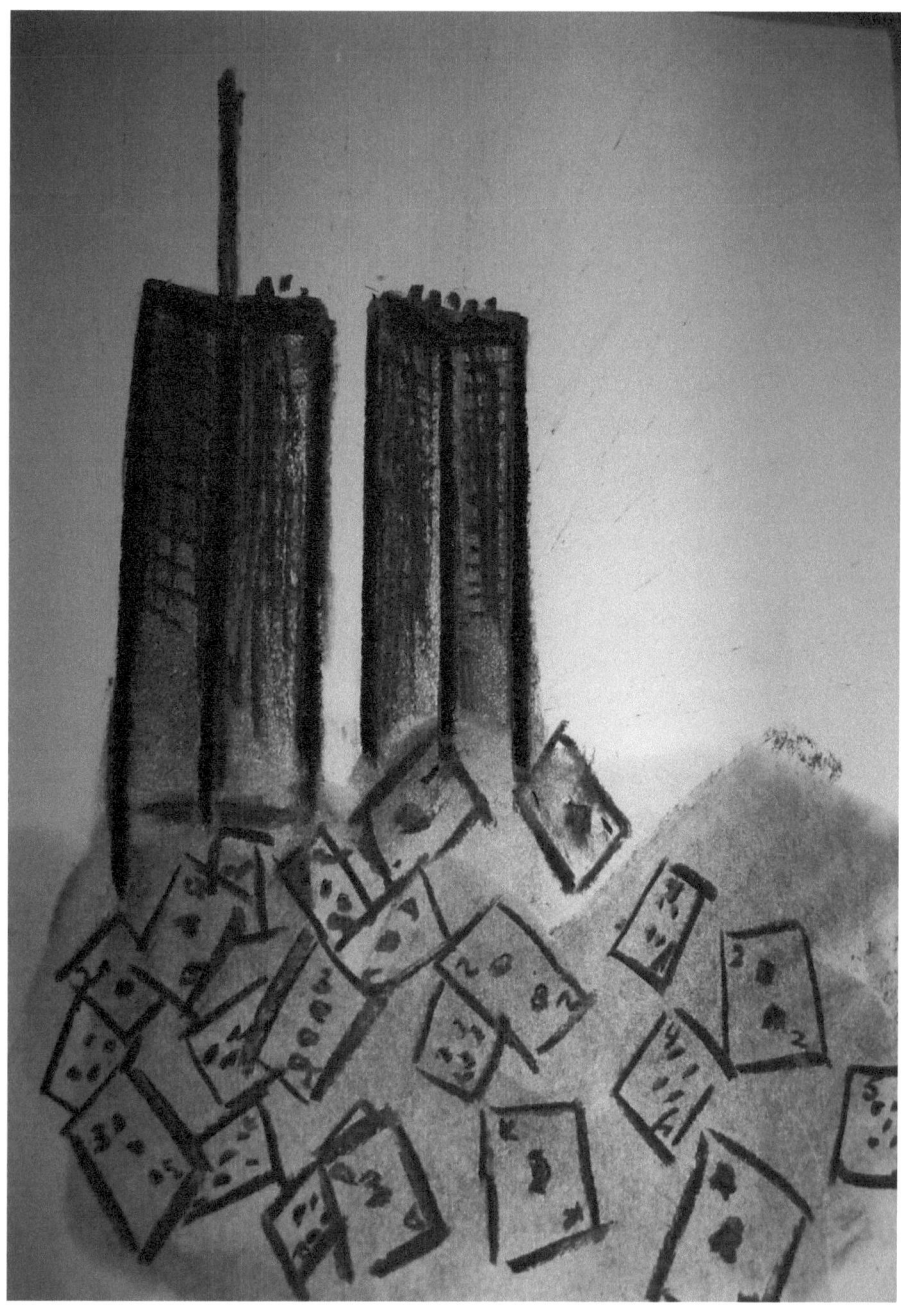

Vibrant Fall

The vibrant change of colors upon the leaves.
As though a veil has been lifted
And the world is suddenly brighter.
Wood-burning stoves fragrant the air.
The geese litter the sky
With their migration south.
I close my eyes and breathe deep.
The smell of maple-wood tingles my senses.
This is the time for shadows to play tricks on us.
This is a celebration of the harvest.
This is the time for All Hallow's Eve.
This is a time for change.
Vibrant yellows, oranges, and reds.
Mixed with the fading shades of greens and browns.
This is Autumn in New England.

10.14.2013

The Hawk in You

I saw a hawk today and thought of you.
I saw a hawk today, soaring wild and free,
While heading to my garden.
I saw a hawk today and thought of you.
I saw a hawk today, high p by the tree tops.
Flying free, wings spread wide.
Gliding along the wind in my backyard.
Regal and free.
I saw a hawk today and thought of you.
I saw a hawk today on my way to my garden.
To pick flowers just for you.
I saw a hawk today and thought of you.

10.15.2013

Better than me

You think that your shit don't stink,
When in fact it reeks like yesterdays trash.
You think that you are king of the hill,
When in fact you are lower than dirt.
You demand all of the respect in the world
But yet you lack the skills to provide any back.
How can you stand way up there?
Upon your lonely throne?
How dare you look down upon me?
Just how do you look at yourself in the mirror?
Do you even see a reflection?
Or are you afraid to even look upon yourself?
Just like Dorian Gray was.
You seem to be lacking in your morals.
While I am drowning in mine.
Oh what a web you weave to have
Those around you tangled in chaos.
It takes two to tango in your game
And I have already left the room.

10.17.2013

The Betrayed

So you are willing to just throw it all away?
All twenty some odd years.
Was it just a game to you?
Was I just a game, a way to pass your time away?
You are choosing to just throw away all the laughs,
The tears and the nothings at alls.
All that thrown away.
As though they are dust upon the wind.
You may have fooled me once before.
But never ever again.
Shall I be fooled by your games again.
All you know is games.
How to play people.
I was you sister.
And you've tossed me aside like yesterday's news.
And played me and others around us.
You had us all fooled.
Until I caught you in the lies.
You think you can talk your way out of this one.
Not a chance, sweetheart.
Don't go looking for me to be there anymore.
I shan't be there anymore.
Nevermore shall I come to your aid.
You played me once, but never again.
Go away fair-weather friend.

Ungrateful sister.
For no longer are you a sister.
You shall have me no more.
Find another to play these games of yours.
For I am done.
And do not care for them any longer.
There is no energy for your petty games and antics.
Find another who will be blind to thee.
For the veil has been lifted.
The mists have parted.
And the vision of mine is clear.
You are no longer to be with me.
I bid thee sister farewell.
I bid thee sister good-bye.
You have betrayed this sacred sisterhood
And betrayed thee for the last time.
No longer do I wish to hear thee's name.
-the betrayed

2.16.2010

Time spent apart brings closer

From the fountains
of forgiveness;
I turn to thee,
Long time friend.
Though the years
May have separated us;
And we are to live
Different lives.
Thy remain my sister
Though our paths
May pull away;
Together
We may thrive.
Though I have
The Innocence Card;
The Dark Queen
Has chosen to keep yours
Hidden from me.
At least for now.
She deems me
Not ready
To view you
At this time.

7.28.2009

Big Courage in a Little Package

Stairs- A challenge.
Not easily over come for her.
Friendships- overwhelmingly powerful.
A smile that brightens up any room.
Who could ever think that such a little thing,
Could be so brave?
Heart needs replacing,
Two years left to live.
Yet, strives strong-
Honor Roll Student.
Still a kid
Still has fun
Still has Hope.
Hope for life
Hope to live
Hope for a cure.
Only a fifth grader
Still has a whole life ahead of her.
And yet, the Fates have decided not for her.
Hope to beat the odds.
Hope for Chance Miracles.

Date unknown